AWAKE

to the

REST OF MY DAYS

Published in 2021 by Birdfish Books
www.birdfishbooks.com

www.kevinsmithpoetry.com

All rights reserved. No part of this edition of this text may be reproduced or transmitted in any form or by any means, electronic or mechanical, including photocopy, recording or any informational storage and retrieval system, without prior permission from the publisher.

Cover images: *Maleny Moon*, by Kate Raffin, and *Death is the Road to Awe*, by Phil Snyder (licensed under CC BY-NC-SA 2.0)

ISBN-13: 978-0-9953718-8-0

Awake

to the

Rest of My Days

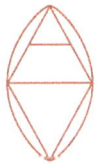

KEVIN SMITH

for Rachael

Acknowledgements

Thirteen Ways of Knowing My Father was commended in the 2018 Newcastle Poetry Prize and published in the competition's anthology, *Buying Online*.

The Mill Road was short-listed in the 2018 Newcastle Poetry Prize and published in the competition's anthology, *Buying Online*; and was runner up in the 2012 Chapter One Promotions Poetry Competition, (London, England).

Death in the Afternoon was long listed in the 2014 Fish Poetry Prize, (County Cork, Ireland); and was published in the Poetic Republic 2013 ebook Publication, (Manchester, England).

Bull was a finalist in the 2012 Aesthetica Creative Writing Competition, (York, England), and was subsequently published in the Aesthetica Creative Writing Annual in York in 2013.

No Southern Boobook was placed 2nd in the 2012 Penumbra Poetry Contest, Tallahassee Writers Association, (Florida, USA); and was short listed in the 2012 Fish Poetry Prize, (County Cork, Ireland). It was subsequently published in the Seven Hills Review in Florida in 2013.

Crows was published in the Poetic Republic 2013 ebook Publication, (Manchester, England).

The Woman on the Bus was highly commended in the 2012 Ethel Webb Bundell Literary Awards, Society of Women Writers, (Western Australia).

Bull was highly commended in 2012 FAWNS Vibrant Verse Poetry Competition, (South Strathfield, Sydney).

Watercourses received an Honourable Mention in the 2012 Adrien Abbott Poetry Prize, (Central Coast, NSW).

A Bedroom in Arles was commended in the 2012 All Poetry Competition, (Nowra, NSW).

The Last Moment was short listed in the 2012 Fish Poetry Prize, (County Cork, Ireland).

Hilltop Station via Wee Jasper was long listed in the 2012 Fish Poetry Prize, (County Cork, Ireland).

Prologue		13
	Killing	15
One:	**Death in the Afternoon**	19
	My Grandfather's Handprint	21
	Bush Funeral	23
	Thirteen Ways of Knowing My Father	24
	My Son the Artist	30
	Watercourses	31
	My Grandmother's Voice, The Rain	34
	pub money	35
	Polly Waffles at the Tumba Café	36
	The Mill Road	37
	Thirty Years On	40
	Last We Heard	41
	How My Father Died	42
	Once Fished	43
	He On the Earth of the Night	47
Two:	**Thirteen Ways of Knowing My Father**	51
	Heron	53
	Up River	54
	Under the Bridge	55
	Crows	56
	Kookaburra	57
	Flight of the Great Egret	58
	No Southern Boobook	59
	Magpies	60
	Winter's Dying Fall	61
	sky regalia	63
	Wollondilly Pelicans	64
	Dreaming White-Bellied Sea Eagle	65
	Death in the Afternoon	66

Three:	**Awake to the Rest of My Days**	**69**
	A Waking Dream	71
	At the Window	72
	Now, What	73
	Portrait of a Young Adventurer	74
	Underground Carpark	75
	Walking into Weather	76
	What Cost	77
	In Need of an Alibi	78
	Next Stop Cheltenham	79
	Where the Days Go	80
	Weather	82
	The Shape of You	83
	Late Night Poem	85
Four:	**The Shape of You**	**87**
	One Slip	89
	At Her Piano	90
	Camels at Eumundi	91
	An Unholy Fire	93
	Minjerribah	94
	That One Day	95
	Breath	96
	Dementia, Suburbia	97
	Market Day	100
	Just One Girl	101
	Hilltop Station via Wee Jasper	102
	End Game	103
	A Bedroom in Arles	104
	The Last Moment	105
	Bull	106
	The Woman on the Bus	107
	Awake to the Rest of My Days	109

Epilogue 111
    Winter Lamb **113**

Notes 115

Prologue

Killing

The sound of steel swiped across steel
brings us kids scuttling out
of the weatherboard house
tucked up in the shade
at the back of the mill.
The old man's honed his blade
for the kill.

He bends over a bundle of wool
jammed between his knees.
A ramrod elbow locks the sheep's
neck across his thigh.
The animal breathes hard.
A keen blade.
The terror in its eyes.

The seven of us stand back
in a cluster and watch the one
sure stroke of the butcher's knife
open the sheep's throat.
Its blood arcs
into the air; the dry earth
drinks it down.

The old man slits the shanks,
inserts the butcher's hook,
hoists the dead weight up
under a limb of gum.
Our brother ropes it off at the trunk.
The carcass swings
as it bleeds. And a cavern

in the sheep's throat
opens and closes like hope—

a mouth, a bottomless pit.
My father strips the hide,
punches it hard where fat sticks.
Bare ribs cradle a hollow
doom. When the knife unzips

the belly,
the hot sludge of guts
spills out, a conglomerate
of blue tumours
mooning over the ground.
Our sticks prod the heavy
nest of intestines.

He severs the liver,
snicks the heart and kidneys
from satchels of fat.
Those shaman's hands—
steeped in blood and sticky
with viscera—
steal into the depth of a thing,

closing in on its emptiness.
Our mother—come from the house—
catalogues the last parts.
In bloodied trousers,
our father splits the skull with an axe
and the cloven bone offers up
tongue and brain.

He cups them in his hands
and drops them
in a bucket of blood.
But it's more dismal work than death
my father's at: he's counting
the chops in his head.
He's dividing each part by nine.

One: Death in the Afternoon

My Grandfather's Handprint

I met him once. He sat
on a stump in the backyard

at my aunt's place when
the evening came down

and a moon bloomed pale.
He was a little man, brittle

as bread crust. The wind
wrestled the last wisps

of his hair, and he could
do nothing but allow it.

He lifted a hand in front
of his face, but the sun

could light no memory there
of stock he'd mustered, or mallee

he'd split by the big river, or traps
he'd laid up in the scrubs. Those hands

worn to forgetfulness had known
no craft of care, of love. And now

history had run dry in them.
His memory of my father gone, too,

perished in the drought lands
that drained the light from this old

man's eyes; the world had become
the desolate place he always knew

it would. His burled hands
like plucked birds perched

on top of his walking stick.
His thin breath barely

stirred the air at his lips. Yet,
somehow it was he who'd left

the deepest impression
in my father's flesh—

handprints branded into
the hide of our lineage.

Bush Funeral Circa 1970

Rastus choked to death when his chain
caught in the wheel of Booshank's ute.
He'd yanked free of my brother's grip
and chased the ute like he always did.
Booshank hit the skids, got out
and said what the bloody hell
were we doing?
                Diane Allum
said a funeral's the thing to do.
'He's a dog,' I said. We dug a hole
in the bush behind the mill and put
dead Rastus in it. She cut some leaves
and told us to collect some stones
to lay along his back. 'What for?'
I said. We shovelled in the dirt.
She lit a fire and danced around
and called out to a sky spirit.
We looked up but couldn't see it.
She said his soul would now float free.
Her tits jiggled under her singlet.
I tried to stop a snigger. She said
we didn't have to cry, about
Rastus was what she meant. We looked
at one another. She left.
                We tied
two sticks together to make a cross
and stuck it in the ground but it
fell over.
        On our way back home
we chucked rocks at one another.
I hit my brother in the head.
When we got home our mother said
we should have had more bloody sense.

Thirteen Ways of Knowing My Father

Where I am going, you cannot come.

— John 13:33

1

The sheep snorted from the back
of the wagon. A clutch of legs roped
together jutted above the back
seat. Butcher's knife and steel
rattled in the footwell.
The smell of sacrifice seeped
into the upholstery as we pulled up
under the killing tree. A butcher's hook
hung above a bloodstained block.
Crows gathered in rags of mourning,
torn from the night. 'Come on', said my father.

2

He was a minor disciple of Christ,
far below a carpenter in
the scheme of things. His vow of poverty
hammered us into a life of privation.

3

On the logging road far
above the mill he fell asleep
at the wheel of the white Falcon.
When it crashed into a mountain
ash the plonk bottle leapt off
the back seat and smacked into
the windscreen moments after my father's
head. He was full of grog,
returning from a fishing trip
with an empty bucket and a busted rod.

4

The bandsaw sang as it carved a canyon
through my father's hand. A sticky
scrawl of blood on sawdust glistened
like icing on a cake. The wound
sutured itself into my dreams.

5

We never knew our father's father.
When he died Dad disappeared
for a week. Mum said nothing and hung
the washing. Us kids swapped looks
then went off hunting Snoopy Warner's
chooks with bows and arrows cut
from wattle saplings. Dad came back
quiet. That night we argued as usual
about who would do the washing up.

6

One of the workers died at the mill.
A log slipped from a winch and he
was pinched to death between two
giant trunks of alpine ash,
his head a red pustule about
to pop. A tree full of kooka-
burras rocked the log yard
with laughter. After, the men milled
around a fire drum in the snow;
they disappeared one at a time
up to the office to talk to the coppers.
Before he was called my father stood
alone blowing into his hands.
That night at the kitchen table an apostle
of silence took its place among us.

7

Friday nights the white Falcon
lurched along the nine miles
of dirt road home. Behind
the wheel my father wrestled with
our fate, his drunkenness a merry-
go-round for our panic, his face a florid
slippery-dip in the dull glow
of the dash. 'Get over, Darl!' my mother
screamed again, and again, her face
contorted in the cracked side mirror
into a circus freak flushed
with horror. Somehow, the slug gun
marksman always got us home.

8

At 51 he lay in a hospital
bed, chest broad and bare,
breath thin, tubes out his nose
a ring of children around him nailed
to their pain. He died anyway.

9

'This meat's off', my brother said.
My father exploded from his chair,
grabbed him by the throat and reefed
him from the table and flogged him hard
and long on the bare floorboards
in front of us all. The house held
its breath. My mother stared ahead,
saw the writing on the wall:
too many mouths to feed, a long-drop
dunny, three kids to a room,
the constant drip of poverty.

10

Us twins bounced across the back
seat of the Falcon as it trucked
and joggled up Back Creek Road.
The rumbling engine filled the no-
man's-land of silence between us
and our father. 'Why don't youse jump
over into the front?' he said.
Me and my brother looked at each other,
weighing up the dangers of being
invited into the inner circle.

11

On fishing trips to the Murrumbidgee
we camped in the bush. Dad dropped
the double bed mattress off
the roof of the Falcon, put the radio
on the bonnet and shot through.

Mum and the girls set up camp.
Us boys trawled the shallows for mussels.

Dad tackled the river, headed
downstream to search for the deep
shady holes. Away from the clamour
of the camp a transenna of silence closed
behind him. My father's faith lay
in setlines anchored to rough-barked
river gums. On an outcrop of bedrock
he settled into silent prayer
to a slippery god: the Murray cod.

12

My father's buried in a dry
cemetery on the edge
of a small country town.
Every five years or so
I go back and walk the stony
tracks between broken headstones.
His black marble slab looms
in full sun. Like a giant's
hand it slaps me back to child-
hood. I'm seven again and small
as a seed on the long
fall from my father the tree.

13

One winter we played in the snow,
my father and his tribe of bastard
children. He'd grab one of us,
shove a snowball down our back
and we'd disappear inside
to the fire. I was the last one
left. And I laughed into
the wind at the sheer joy
of having him to myself at last.

My Son the Artist

His drawing is a coloured bog.
In his hand a red nib—
bright as his head of hair—hammers

open the stratosphere of the page.
The sun pours in; grey rays erupt
from a crimson ring. Something princely

wakens in him; his fingers stiffen.
A dragon, a blazing yellow fable,
orange legs and a milk-white tail,

stalks his apocalypse. A blue-
eyed viper hangs in an impasto
sky, the red sun smoking its tail,

its head cocked to plunge into
the labyrinth. The queen dead,
shadows darken the pale discs

of the artist's eyes. His hand
rises. The red nib forges swords
against the marshalling forces

and draws on ruptured battlements
the one to lead them on—his red
hair rising like a sun.

Watercourses

> 'First wonder goes deepest.'
>
> —Yann Martel, *Life of Pi*

i

The watercourses of my childhood
were thin clear creeks with fluted
chutes, tongued smooth into bedrock
we'd slide down into shallow pools,
the rock pocked with sinkholes and shafts
honed by pebbles over volumes
of time.   These aching arteries carved
paths into stone we ran our hands
over, over and over again,
in blind attempts at reading the braille
of water prints.   A choir of creeks
sang anthems to the arcane; ancient
cycles of song rippled through
the rivers of our veins. Tunes rose
like smoke through leaves of alpine ash.
Flat on our backs in long-tongued
grass, we counted out loud the dragon-
clouds that drifted from blue realms
and blazed above the hardwood mill
pounding like a foundry on the dark
side of hell, the millstream

a minstrelsy of crotchets and quavers,
a cadence of dark vatic revelation.

ii

The watercourses of my childhood
were small incessant things, their necks
chock-a-block with smooth flat stones.
They trickled into scant dams
flat as cowpats, panoptic discs
set in low-slung paddocks.
                         We sank
knee deep into slick cold mud,
our scrawny arms flung under
a blistering sun. The stones sat snug
as guns in our hands.[1]
                     We skimmed them across
the dam, each stone-skip dwindling
as it went.
           Our faces lay in pools
of sky mirrored blue
in this dark glass eye to eternity.
Log trucks ploughed the dry road home
and haystacks of dust bloomed after
they'd gone.
              We looked up from the creek,
our bare feet slipping over cold rock.
We chased crayfish through translucent
wombs, their blue claws scrabbling over
russet-coloured stones.
                    Far off
the hooter in the mill cried out,

a voodoo chant among the trees,
an opus of voltage quickening our dreams.

iii

The watercourses of my childhood
ran untethered through farmland and scrub,
stony creeks that undercut banks,
gouged bolt-holes where trout hid.
Their speckled backs gleamed in glassy
streams, ice-cold throbs that torpedoed
through our hands.
Too quick to tickle
onto the bank with chilblained fingers,
they sluiced the slippery rock; their knowing
pulsated in our guts like a belly-flop
over a crest in the mill road
when the school bus lumbered to carry
us home.   The creeks' lilt and tempo
swirled through the bush like an early morning
mist and eddied round log piles
stacked at the mill, riffled our
marrow and sang up our souls.
And under thousands of acres of stars
we nested in the innocence
of what we were.   The creeks played
requiems to a waning moon,

the tunes purling into the mill-blind
night, each note lit like a firefly.

My Grandmother's Voice, The Rain

I wake to find rain has come in the night. At the window
it's falling still—softening the earth and making the morning

tender—and the morning tenderises me. It slows me
into myself, a place I rarely go. It's rough

country, mine shafts and hard sunlight—a lithosphere
of bruise and antique hurt. I lie in bed and listen

to the rain dance its cadence on the tin, her fables
a mute articulation of another world

entire.[2] The rain speaks like a grandmother I never had—
tempting me to the edge of myself. I close my eyes,

imagine a grandmother sitting on my bed. 'Rest now,
child.' Soft against my cheek, her fingers—gloved

in translucent skin—seek the blood in me. Her song
lulls me to sleep, cradled in tenderness. I wake—again—

to truth: both grandmothers dead before they knew
I'd come into the world. My tongue searches, blind

for their names. 'Be kind to your soul', these grandmothers say
and stroke, like rain, a gathered providence in me.

pub money

blunt hands cut and calloused hung
beside trousered legs in grog-clogged
air that pushed against the walls and small
windows of this cramped damp pub.
thigh high i was, watched by
the red eyes of fag ends as i cut
my way blindly through the closely planted
legs of timber men. i'd drawn the short
straw to see who'd fail in the next attempt
to snig the old man from a smoke-choked
friday night with mates. they'd slugged their guts
out at the mill all week and couldn't wait
to forget. they murdered middies like outlaws
on the run.
                   as i came close i saw
my father's hand dive into his pocket.
i looked up at him, chin tilted
toward the ceiling, and waited. an outsider.
the talk was packed tight. my eyes dropped;
it seemed his arm ended at the wrist.
nothing existed below. no finger. no hope.
as if his bushranger's hand had been blown clean off
by a martini-henry in a battle
with the traps. below the nothingness coins
danced in his trouser pocket, the clinking like rain
on tin to a boy lost in the sahara.

outside my mother sat in the car—ambushed
by the cold—and tried to knit the winter
away. the streets were empty except for us
seven kids and our small voices dumb
to income and how it came and went.

Polly Waffles at the Tumba Café

To my father

Have I given you too hard a time
since your death? Have I forgotten the footy
carnivals you took us to in Wagga;
or how you lifted backyard cricket
to euphoria striding to the wicket
to bowl your off-spinners ready or not; and how
the drink softened you for a time?
What if we'd been boys together? Would I
have understood you better if we'd set
the mill yard on fire and filched the peaches
from Snoopy Warner's tree and tried to steal
the Polly Waffles from the Tumba café?
Would I have run and left you with the guilt?
Or stood my ground and said it's not your fault?

The Mill Road

He woke in charcoal dark and put
his work clothes on in the narrow
passage between the iron bed
and the wardrobe's brown veneer.
She stirred, sat up and wiped sleep
from her eyes, and the window, where
she looked, was a black vault open
on eternity. She reached
for her dressing gown and felt
the coming dawn.
                       The boy held
his bedroom door ajar. The father
walked past and flicked the switch.
A dull yellow filled the gloom,
and the boy drew back into his room.

In the laundry, the father splashed
freezing water on his face.
The pipes groaned like a loaded
winch. He took a towel from
the nail beside the window opaque
with frost. The blank face of some
bespoke future.
                       She packed the fire-
box with ironbark and opened
the flue, took a pan from
a hook above the stove. As
she dropped tea into a pot
he rolled a smoke and checked for snow.

At the stove he put his arms
around her. She nudged him off to chop
an onion and fry an egg. She cooked
porridge for the clutch of kids who filled
bare rooms with sleeping breath.

At the back door he pulled
his work boots on. They looked at one
another. He stepped outside and cold
air bullied its way in;
she woke the kids for school.
                              They crowded
the stove. 'Where's your brother?' At
the window he watched his father foot-
slog the mill road, a dank shadow
cuffed to a reprobate sky.
He snuck out the back door.
The mother at the dishes. 'Where
are you goin'?' The door banged
shut.
         His father's boots left prints
in icy sludge. He jumped from print
to print and landed short each time
but kept on trying. The hooter sounded
at the mill. The father turned
and saw the boy at his game.
'Go on home for Christ's sake!'
Some mute thing stood between them.
'I said get home!'
                         A log truck buckling
under its load crawled the bend
out of a cloud-drowned world.
Brute metal and beheld
momentum shouldered cold air
from the road. Its roar mauled
the quiet. The boy leapt aside.
The truck pushed on toward the mill.
A rag flapped from the longest log:
a hand shredded red or
the sacrament of a forsaken god.
The boy looked back to the house, then down

to the mill.
                It had no walls; machinery
shivered in the wind. The twin
blades of the Canadian—tall as a man—
stood in silhouette against
a reluctant dawn. Blitzes idled
in cold air, doorless, with no
windscreens, waiting for the day
to begin. Men—cryptic in
the mist—walked the yard to warm
their hands at fire drums. The boy
lobbed a knot of wood into
a bank of smouldering bark—opened
it up like a saw cut. Vermilion
coals flared in a colourless landscape.
The father turned. Beyond, smoke
dribbled from chimneys, the houses a sniffling
cluster of chilblained boxes. 'Go on
the hell home for the last time,'
he said, and followed the men into
the mill.
              The overseer stood
fast—arms folded and face
hard against the cold—and waited
for the boy to go.
                  The Blitzes skidded
in the muddy yard. The Canadian whined
to life, searching blindly to find
momentum to flitch the first log
of the morning. Above the mill smoke
bloomed white.
                  The day got colder; the boy
turned for home. On the mill road
his father's footprints—the few that remained—
went one way, the boy's another.

And the sky dropped its basket of snow.

Thirty Years On

After Ted Kooser

You'd be eighty-six today if
you'd lived.³ And what might we have looked like
walking streets I've rarely seen since I left town,
left you? On a sunlit Saturday—
thirty years since your death—you'd buy
the paper, check the guide for runners at
Randwick, eye the pub we passed. You'd ask
about my son and I imagine pride—
burning in your eyes—rise from a place
I'd not known. You never met him though.
But you knew his name and shared a ward with him—
after your fall. I stood at your bed; he lay
in a bassinet not yet a fortnight old
his breath catching on life—and yours on death.

Last We Heard

Clouds subdue this late summer heat.
I've spent the day mowing grass and trimming
fruit trees that outgrow themselves—and I feel
no better for it. From this window I watch
sunlight break into the yard. I put
my empty cup on the desk, re-enter silence—
an intruder in this room where my son
once slept; these shelves accrue the residue
of his years here. A Buddha statue his mother
left him after her death stares at me
—my only defence, to turn away. I wonder
what she'd think. And what might she have done.
A son so at odds with self he could
not sense the love he might become. Could she?
This talk undoes me. He's on the streets—last
I heard: if love knows life has been hard
enough,[4] why is she set against him? And why
—when I wake from sleep—is sleep the thing
I lack the most? As I lack the crux
of love—the seed incised from the peach.

How My Father Died

Leaving the RSL late one night
my father tripped on death. As the poker game nudged
the small hours of morning he and the boys
moved on to bourbon.
                       He fell down a flight
of stairs as he left. His head bounced twice
on concrete steps, his body slumped to a standstill
at the bottom.
                The boys left later and saw
him lying there, passed out from too much drink
is what they thought. They threw him in the back
of his Datsun and drove him home and left him.

At dawn, my mother, leaving for work, saw
him sprawled in the back of the car like a pile of old
blankets. Spiders of morning light crawled
the folds of his unconsciousness. She left
him, too.
            Hours later my sister—smoking
a cigarette—saw him from the porch.
She lifted the tailgate and rolled him over. Two
black eyes blared at her like festival trumpets.
He'd been bashed, she thought, and called the ambulance.
They rushed him to hospital in a coma.

On the fourth day we got the call:
'You'd better come over.' The rain leaked
from the winter sky and trees shivered
in a wind. We shuffled into the lift.
On the fifth floor the doors opened
—a clunking curtain, the final act. My sister
rushed into the arms of her audience
bawling her single line: 'He's gone. He's gone.'

Once Fished

1

We cast our lines over still
water and the sinkers plop
like sheep droppings onto the glass-
like surface. And are swallowed. Ripples
radiate toward the dam's edge
like hours. And we wait.

2

Magpies, with cackling calls, poke
mullock at our stupid inactivity,
but we're only nine and it can't last.
We throw stones at the heckling
codgers, unroosting them from their high
perches in almighty gums. Their wings
crank them into the distance.
Pale blue relentless sky. Cows
tread soft in sodden paddocks.
Tugging grass. Listlessly.

3

Three and a half miles down
the stony road in a curtained
kitchen my mother wipes the knife
on her apron. Fat spits
in the saucepan. Blowflies clog
the air. Rigid heat.

4

We skip stones over the surface
of the dam, bored shitless
with fishing and its unrewards.
We lift earth-stained rocks—sucked
from mud and cowpats—and heave
them with thin-armed might into
the dam. The gut-drodging swallowed
sound echoes across far
paddocks. Cows lift their heads.
Crows cry. Pale blue relentless sky.

5

In the distance, smoke rises
from the burner. The men at the mill
—my old man among them—sweat
and wrestle the timber until the dead-
owled hooter sounds out 'smoke-o!'
They sit on bench tops. Squat in patches
of shade. Cigarettes hang from wrinkled
lips. They talk, silence between
each thought, scrawling the sawdust.

6

Then the rod bends and the sickening
excitement of hooking a fish thumps
us in the midriff. We cut our way
through noon-day heat and snatch the rod.
Hawk-eyed boys looking in deep.
Searching out the fish. There!
There! It darts and stops and starts
straining the invisible line in vain.
We jerk it into sudden air
and bash out its brains on a rock.

7

The knife tears through scales and cold
flesh like old carpet. We rip
the fish from anus to gullet.
Fingers scoop the oozing warmth
of tiny innards and plop them in
the dirt. An invitation to smitten
flies. An empty fish rolls
an empty eye. Pale
blue relentless sky.

8

We chuck the fish in a hessian bag
and plug it below the water's surface.
Its guts lie on the bank, a tangled
mass of stillborn secrets. Innocent
fingers probe the bruised heap—
kidney, intestine, little liver
all laid bare. The heart still pumps!
A skinny finger jabs the tiny
mass and all is still—a second
death. Another jab and the heart
starts over, longing for its sodden
body lying at the bottom of
the bank. The game goes on.
Resurrection after resurrection.
Stop. Start. Live. Die.

He on the Earth of the Night[5]

the sea is mouthing at the shore.

a man, alone, is fishing off the rocks.

beyond the break a surfer straddles his board and the ocean
rolls under him, and he waits—a world away—for the right

wave. me here on the shore replete with rage.

i want the sea to come and take me, and tip me off the edge
of everything, this everyday grey sky. my son sits next to me

mute with anxiety, his hair a dull fire, the machinery of his

mind relentless in its iron-blind drive to shunt him to a place

he won't be coming back from soon.
for the twentieth time today he asks if i'm ok and i could weep.

he gets up and moves away.
he walks the hard sand along the tideline, belted by the wind.

there's nowhere else he can go.

and i'm empty of ideas.

so i wait, and i'll wait an age. i listen, but the sea's got no

answers; its mumbled sermons collapse the shore and make
atheists of us all.

and the wind, a bitched hyena, drools over the schadenfreude
i feed it.

and the beach is a cunt,

and the sun dumb and homeless—bereft—a dream pounded
to death by the waves, the sky. the hollowness of it all.

don't ask me any more how he is.

don't tell me anymore what you think is going on with him.

don't share your wisdom, your professional opinion,

your considered response to what he said to you in the half
hour you sat with him in hospital, and think you could know

anything of him at all. while i,

i go home and live every moment with him, each day dragged
by the hair across the rough terrain of seconds and minutes

and hours, and then on into the uncertain country of the rest

of my life with him, scaling his psychosis,

his neurosis, or whatever name you want to give it

—the unknown geomorphology of his soul you want to flatten
with a label and glue to a corflute sky. you miss

the calderas and canyons, the rock falls

of torment and epiphany, the hammered sky hammering him,
and the night sky split by lightning, its secular power,[4] its thin

fingers, finding out his darkness, his love, and this wretched

vulnerability that takes him too far down

—into cold caves and their gravelled streams, their winding,
vaclusian, down into the dumb earth, its billions of years

of wrack and thrust—where he might find a place to be.

as if the earth didn't have enough on her seismic plates.

but there my son might rest—so far down into darkness
so pure he could almost call it a friend. i wonder if

i'll ever see him escape the caverns of himself,
and those rock layers you keep laying over him with your

prognoses, your predictions, your judgments calved

from an ice-sheet of ignorance. i'll tell you,
this boy's a mystery, not a condition. he's a laccolith;

he's the tectonic shift, the surge
and cataclysm of himself, a blindness—urgent and hurting—

ripening in desire to breach mantle and crust, and thrust out
into the moonlit quiet of the undiscovered soul,

the wind singing into him,
the sound of the sea, profound as sleep, lulling him onto

the shores of himself: he, himself, the answer:

a fire ignited, blazing like truth.

and we—now—blinded by him, sublime in himself
on the earth of the night, the moon running through

his translucent soul illuminating
that thing in him we couldn't see

that cried in silence: *this is me.*[7]

Two: Thirteen Ways of Knowing My Father

Heron

She could be a statue: her neck—like rolled metal—
thinning toward the sky,
her beak planing for union with sunlight.
The only patch of whiteness on her beds a dark eye.
                    Her legs as thin as pencils.

Then she moves; her feathered rump wobbles like a duck's.
Her neck pulses—soft decibels of ache. A pocket giraffe
in blue motion, she sifts
through the undergrowth like smoke—as if she were
                    its vapour—nudging

leaves with her beak, her grazing elegant as a breeze.
She walks in garlands of ease, flight folded
into her wings. Blades of lomandra
bow as she passes—her existence an eternity of simple things.

Up River

Between the wharf buildings
—beyond the broad beam
of the river I can just see—
houses crouch on the hillside.
Smoke rises from chimneys.
Above them a dark stain of trees
and a sky aching with cloud—
a bruised wall the sun stumbles
behind. A lone gull lumps
upstream pushing long into icy
wind and my heart bleeds blue
all over the known world as the gull
takes me up the sunless river
and brings me home again
into the warm fires of myself.

Under the Bridge

I stop on the bridge and listen to the river stroke stones
into a more rounded notion of themselves, wishing

it was me. A white-faced heron appears beneath
blue quandongs and rose gums—as if from centuries

of shadow—looking more at peace with the world than I'll
ever be. She steps into herself—into the river—

and inspects her beat. An epoch of studied prudence, she lifts
her feet where sunlight shatters water. Leaves freckle

still pools. Her beak unpicks the shoals, needling
for small fish or frogs, and if she misses out

it doesn't matter; the river will offer something else;
stress is not her thing. She takes the river for what

it is and the river's better for it. She stills, her legs
bent to neat angles by the vice of refracted light.

A statue cast in nickel and brass, she waits. Her head
tilts. And something trickles in. With slick precision,

she cracks the shallows, glucks the fish down her throat,
a glint of silver, and walks on water, a trick of light

—and the lift and pulse of shadows over a broken surface.

Crows

The crows gallop through a posse of clouds
and dismount in the poincianas. Their black
coats glisten in the brooding heat,
each bird a knotted hieroglyph. One drops
to the grass and washes itself under a sprinkler
in the shade. I throw him a scrap of meat.
His henchmen, fidgeting in the trees, ride
shotgun on the sun that slides towards
noon, the dead air a stalemate
of probable cause. I watch the crow watch me
—the black kernel of its eye an ancient
seed. He, a dim premonition
loosed on the city.
                    He looks to the meat.
Shakes his head. Clicks his beak. Ignores
the bait—an apostate from the church of reason.
His gang of cubist gunslingers hobble
closer and flap in agitation, itinerants
lingering on civility's rim. I move
toward him.
           Wings crack like gunshots
as the crows mount the air. Their shadows spill
from the sky and run loose down streets
and across the tiled roofs that truss the suburbs.

Kookaburra

Its chortling
cracks
the dawn open.

A split beak
tips up
into yolks of sunlight.

Gripped
in a sudden
stillness

the bird,
a chunk of bark
grafted to a black wattle,

chronicles
the lunacy
of the parliaments of knowledge,

its eye
an aperture
into burls of lore

fermented in a darker wood.
That beak,
dull invincible teak,

honed wisdom that doesn't speak,
laughs hard
at a cuckold world.

Flight of the Great Egret

I stand on the edge of the lake and watch a great
egret fly low across the still water with
an ease impossible to fake. Reflected
on the surface, its twin echoes a simple purpose.
                                                   The bird
slides its neck forward—a trombone sliding perfect
tones—to reach into a single future rippling
the air, the air it now inherits. Its twin—
of the same mind—reaches, too, as if both
were fledged for this migration, loosed from any other
reasoning.
                At the end of the lake, the bird
gains altitude—almost without effort—
above the bulrushes and the conifers, until
it clears the ridge and is gathered in
by a white sky—and is made, suddenly,
so much the whiter for it.
                              In travelling, the bird fathoms
itself as I never have; in my reflection,
I see something at odds. Evening lays tranquility
over the lake, and shadows—like floodwater—rise
up the trunks of eucalypts.
                        I walk away,
not quite knowing where I might lead myself.

No Southern Boobook

After Bronwyn Lea

It used to be[8] he nested in a tree
down on the driveway,

his wings folded in a hangar
hung in a bower of limbs and leaves.

His gaze—half alarm, half
wonderment—gripped us with talons

that cruelled the fur of small marsupials.
One morning we checked the bower

for his brown and white speckled face.
We found small bones of emptiness

in his place. Down the road
we listened for his call—

a spooked hoot like a smoke puff
drifting through the undergrowth.

But the air has forgotten him,
harbinger of storms. We look

for him rummaging under the clouds
somewhere and easing into his freedom—

a truant shooting the moon. And when
the rain comes we turn for home,

the wind in the bloodwoods
keening for his song.

Magpies

Suddenly there are magpies in the yard.
In the mornings they step through damp grass,
arms tucked out of harm's way.
Their beaks stab the wet ground;
they tug worms—those earth-packed sausages—
out of smooth dark tunnels.

Their heads dip like pump jacks
on a west Texas oil field,
the black and white of their jackets
borrowed from a nun's habit

or from cows sauntering to the dairy at dawn—
milk and oil spills on a green paddock.

Winter's Dying Fall

In winter's dying fall—
             these last days of August—a gum empties
         itself of sulphur-crested cockatoos
who, like anti-refugee protestors, scream at me
                         to go home, not knowing

that this is where I come from. They might have
                     been nuns once—so clean their
         habits—until a pagan god set them
in this high country, a handful
                 of miles from where I went to school.

Iced-over dams—winter's glaucous
                 eyes—melt under each day's new-made
         sun, the cockatoos his fraught
children, a rabble impatient
         for spring's harvest of saffron thistle. From the house

I hear them still. The wind howls
                         in the chimney and this old place
         creaks its story of winters survived
and the scars laid on it by each. All at once
                 I feel the frailty of its aged bones.

The cockatoos, in stringy barks,
     now settle into respectful silence, more at home here
       than any of us
have ever been. The wind freshens
                 and lifts iron, loose on a roof, that baffles

and clangs across the paddocks
                     and sets the cockatoos off again,
         their cries mournful now as a bitch
whose pups have been taken from her. From the trees
                 the birds explode like confetti.

In the wind they move like
        a school of fish deep in blue sky. They roost again,
    and blossom in
a wintered elm. They could be ice crystals
                or clumps of snow and nothing

else could make me feel
        more at ease but a distant horizon, a cloudless
    sky come down to my knees
—the clamour of the cockatoos sounding
                all the world like applause.

sky regalia

white cockies
bright as unicorns
plunder the kingdom of the sky

they hurl their curled claws
against the fortress walls of gravity
hijacking the headwinds

they catapult
festoons of cloud
they knot the rollicking air

with crested buffoonery
and joust and jester westward
on a clavichord of calls

then fade
into the absence
their baubled laughter leaves

Wollondilly Pelicans

When evening closes in, we camp on the Wollondilly
south of Oberon. A pod of cockatoos,
                                  frocked in glossy black,
preach from a pulpit of eucalypts set high on a ridge.
Fresh scabs of rock have fallen from the cliff face
that backdrops two pelicans
                         as they descend to contour-fly
the river, divining the hull of themselves through each

reach of elastic air. Neck and
                          neck, their porcelain gullets breast
the day's final light. They glissade a thin cushion of air
between themselves and the water—such low-level flying,
a koan they resolve in one
                    sweep of the river. They rise like pale
monks, and the sky unlocks its temple doors
                             to a sacrosanct silence,
an evening wind chanting through the she-oaks.

Dreaming White-Bellied Sea Eagle

The air is your element, the earth mine.
You take the wind and work it in your favour.
Dipping your wings to casuarinas, you ride
the offshore updrafts: all that vision, all
that grace—
          and I think of you, my son,
sedated on a hospital bed. You booked
a ticket—with a handful of pills—
to a country far from consciousness. If you'd
told me you were leaving I'd have brought
you here and hoped the syntax of this bird's flight
found its way into your story and changed
the course it took—and how it ended. Here,
on this country's rim, you might have found
a hero's diction—each word a step
into a heart you'd not yet learned to love.

Death in the Afternoon[9]

I brake hard but can't avoid hitting the bird—
a soft thud on the windscreen. A slack of feathers tumbles

through the rear-view mirror. I turn back to find
the small parcel of her body slid between an envelope

of road and sky, her breast upturned—a burst of yellow
kindling on the cold expanse of dark tar. I stop

the car beside her in the middle of the road, hoping
she's dead, that a log truck won't come over the hill—out

of this wasteland—and add me to the carnage. I open the door
and there she lies flat on her back. Her matchstick legs

mime a slow up-side-down bicycle ride.
Her beak opens and closes—a simple mechanical device

engineering a soundless cry—her eyes locked open
in shock, flight bumped from her wings. I see the pink

nest of guts slip down her plumage, leaking heat
into the cold road. I raise my boot above the bird

and know I've got to bring it down hard. After,
I lift her body from the tar—to spare her the merge

into the bitumen's midnight black, its quiet oblivion—
and I lay her in a nest of grass. And now the rain

sweeps in veils across the granite plateau over
this one-man funeral, one small death in the afternoon.

Three: Awake to the Rest of My Days

A Waking Dream

I woke in dark and left our bed without
waking her, to come into this room

and write what's on my mind. And find it's you.
I picture you in bed—a thousand miles

south of here. I'm standing in your room
to watch your breath fall and swell,[10] your husband's

arm draped across your waist. I think
to touch you—my fingers on your skin—that you

might wake and slip from bed, and lead me
to your kitchen where I'd watch you make the tea.

We'd talk sotto voce at the table
till light prised the glass from your window.

At the Window

Suppose I'm sitting at the window
in this kitchen waiting for the rain to come
and thinking of you. Thunder wakes the clouds
and birdsong gladdens the bush, and far beyond,
a chainsaw's muted growl. When I see
the date—the thirteenth of October—I try
to remember: is this your birthday? Does it really
matter, I wonder—you're a thousand miles
away. Suppose you're wondering about me,
and why I haven't called. My face darkens
in the window as the storm beguiles
the light from the room. Suppose things
had been different—that I'd left her instead
of you. Suppose we had that child, that life—
the one that we conceived, so full of poems
about those things we'd fathomed in each other.
Would you be happy now with how it turned
out? Would I? Sometimes, I let myself
imagine the way we'd have kissed, waking each day,
and how you'd have let me find my way between
your thighs, the rain at the window, thinking of her.

Now, What

After Raymond Carver

Make use of the things around you.[11] This city you
don't live in, its tiled
                     roofs tilting into late sun, antennas
clinging to chimney stacks dribbling incoherence down
dark cables. A car door slamming.
                                  An aeroplane hanging
white ensigns in the sky. And this woman

you once loved lying on a bed in a hotel room you'll
never see again. Strange
                  how you overcome the temptation
to step out onto the balcony and grip the balustrade,
knuckles whitening, vertigo's
                        hands tightening around your
neck—and you swooning over a quick death.

Portrait of a Young Adventurer

There's a black and white photo of you
on my bedroom wall taken over
twenty years ago. Under the dust
you reek of India and gleam with freedom.
You're standing in a shallow lake outside
the walls of Jaisalmer, dressed in a *salwar
kurta*[12] watering your camel, the one
you'd learn soon enough was half wild;
later she would throw you. You're poised to toss
the reins over her head, your grip on her
frail as the nose-peg through her nostril.
At the last moment she shoved her head
toward the camera, as if she'd sensed a trap.
But you did not. The camera clicked a split
second before she reached her freedom
in a country beyond the frame. She, too, was caught
inside the portrait of what you could have been.

Underground Carpark

We walk into the mouth of an underground
carpark—that no one you know might see us.
The air's suffused with diesel fumes and muffled
noise from streets above. We step around
the words we told ourselves we wouldn't say.
Our bodies' wants could not be silenced though:
I find your hand in mine as concrete walls
close in. You turn to me and we hold on
to one another until it becomes a thing
we ought not do. I have no answer for
your eyes, nor you for mine. Footsteps spill
down stairs. We pull apart—a flush of shame
mirrored on our faces. A door opens.
Light pins our shadows to the wall,
these truant selves in want of heart, of voice,
incapable of love, so freed from choice.

Walking into Weather

The weather is about the house. Clouds
                squeeze the last light from the sky
and a west wind starts up and rain hammers the roof.
In the dark, downpipes
         choke on too much of a good thing. Inside, stone
walls hold the line between me and the primordial:
I walk into the weather
           anyway. She—scented and elegant as a lover—
throws her misty cloak about me

and I think of you, that you've spent the day at school,
                now home, perplexed by the metrics
       of the mundane. And I wonder why your being
    there—in a life so far from mine—is air
and light to me. I picture you
             —the last time we met—
                  in a floral dress, and how it flounced
       your form and spoke so eloquently

of your hips, your calves—and how
               it lit a fire in your eyes. Beyond them
blackness too great for reckoning—a darker wind.
I walk the midnight into your eyes
                and leave myself further behind
                      —deaf to rain in the trees—
the wind blind to reason. And I try
       to sense you there—breathless in the dark—
                          that I might go on.

What Cost

I wake at dawn—camped beside a river—
and find you in my head. Roos emerge
from mist, while in my mind a darkened room—
you lying on a bed; light fell through
the window as your skirt rose up your thigh.
Mirrored in the glass, our twins look in
on the life—back then—that time forbade us.
I touch your lips, and your thighs unfold;
your eyes shut fast, that you might deny
—later on—that I was there at all.
When your tongue swims in my mouth like ether
through the stars, you slide onto my fingers
and I search the dark for something lost—
for what might be redressed—and at what cost.

In Need of an Alibi

The rain, wet with mischief, has come and gone
all day—casing the house, the yard, the bush—
the sun as heedless as a thief in need
of an alibi. She's in the garden
gleaming in her red jacket, taking
odds against the rain she knows is coming,
hurrying in the last plants as gloom
breaks into the yard—as welcome as a cache
of unpaid bills. She strips weeds from garden
walls, unmasking clusters of cherry tomatoes,
red as a drunk's eyes and just as swollen.
Rain comes. She chats to the cat—coiled
on the couch beside the window, dreaming
sunlight—comforting as wads of dollar bills.

Next Stop Cheltenham

A woman leans against a post and smokes
a cigarette. Another—in black stockings
and spiked heels—hauls a case grievous
as freedom. A recorded voice warns me to stay
behind the line, and the train arrives.
I get on. Next stop Cheltenham, I'm told.
Sandstone wears graffiti here—names,
promises. A train roars by on a parallel line.
Metal poles flick past and tabulate
the distance to the bridge above the station
where we parted. But the feel of you—
when I pressed your dress and felt the heat—
endures. Did you gift me something then—
that I might not return, or not know when?

Where the Days Go

The day wakes with sleep on its mind and in its eyes.
Catbirds call it to attention—and you and I from bed—

that they might put things to rights in a world
full of things out of sorts with themselves.

When we walk up the drive—the dog trailing us—
we list our aches and pains and the sun writes a fresh

history of the world, and things begin not to be so bad.
This basalt, eighteen million years young, we've built

our lives on binds us. The last days of October
ripen fruit on trees you planted three seasons back.

The mulberry offers handfuls of berries that blood
our fingers and our tongues, and the dog's eyes

blaze with hope. He and I walk deeper
into the morning—testing the future with each step—

and you turn back. The red and yellow fruit on trees
become parrots and fly, and I wonder at my life's

transformation, which has given me more
than should have been possible. I wait in shade;

the dog's tongue lolls wet in warm air. I weigh
the swollen tumour in my palm and try not to think

how little time he has left. I find you pulling weeds
and laying hay beneath your apricot tree, enticing

poetry from dry earth. You see me coming—
slowed for an old dog—and your eyes reach into mine

the way sunlight falls through water. How is it ageing
could be elegant as egrets grazing beneath black cattle—

a play of snow and shadow? You gift me a look
that lays bare the truth of yourself,

and something opens in me; and I realise
you're most of what I've wanted all my life.

The sun shepherds the day over the range, over the woods
and open pastures, and blues the sky. The dog lies in dust

and closes his eyes, and October's warmth
takes him into the back country of sleep.

Weather

The weather has been crying all day—
sometimes sniffling, sometimes bawling. Now
it's a steady sob as if she knew
a pain that had no end. All day I've been
inside the house writing and drinking tea.
The sun has fallen from the sky and evening
closes like a heavyweight's eye. The trees
stoop like old men at a funeral staring
at the ground; the clothesline has lost its will
to live. Clouds lurk, gate-crashers at
a party: trouble's coming but you don't
know when. Beneath the leaden cloud a light
bleeds; when a quiet descends into the room
the lack of her opens a wound.

The Shape of You

I try not to think of you without
    thinking it so. Then the rain comes
        and I close the door to the world
            beyond my door, and you arrive,

Alive in me. You led me on
    a walk along the harbour foreshore,
        the sandstone steps hard
            as the resolve we thought we had.

We climbed and when the list
    and roll of your hips fell under my
        touch, a joy came calling—sweeter
            than the water lying in the bay,

Or the breeze that dowsed the heat
    from our bodies, from the shore.
        We swam at a small beach after
            changing on the street between the car's

Doors. You chose to wear your one-piece,
    and I learned of you that when the ocean
        floor's beyond your reach a fear takes you
            —that something from imagined depths

Will rise—uninvited—beside you.
    Your smile strained when I slowed my stroke.
        On the footpath, we exchanged a lozenge
            —from your tongue to mine. You walked

On and laughed it off as child's
    play. But I could not. Your skirt
        shipped across your thighs and told
            your form like waves tell the sea.

I open the window to put you outside
my mind, and I'm taken—by a wet sky
—beyond the given world. And there I find
an ache inside myself the shape of you.

Late Night Poem

At four a.m. I wake to a late-night poem
tapping in my head. I slide from bed—
careful not to wake her—and piss outside,
my urine unspooling syntax on wet grass.
Bats fly over—trailing a wake of stars.[13]
I close the door of my writing room. Screen
light from my laptop burns bright in the dark;
my ears ring the quiet. I imagine a moon—
beyond a wall of cloud—hawking the dawn.
Even the trees don't stir. An hour writes
a blank page. When I get back to bed
she's still asleep and I rest my hand
on her hip. Pouring through the glass
from deep space, starlight bathes her face.

Four: The Shape of You

One Slip

It should never have ended
like this. A light press of her foot:
the wheel hub locks into place—
and there would have been
no frontpage story, no photo
of the lake. Her phone rings;
she answers—and words flood
her ear. She looks into the tree-
tops, sweeps a loose strand of hair
from her face. The moments roll
away. She turns back and the pram
is gone. The call goes out—a child
abducted, they think. Word spreads.
Eyes sweep the park and beyond.
For too short a time, folded blades
of grass tell the route it took. Soon,
the theory of abduction runs dry—
urgency stills. People stand round
in clumps; whispers pool in the shade.

Eyes turn toward the lake. A man
in a wetsuit wades in. Those few
wet steps: a hip against a handle
so close to the shore. Like an old-
world Mephisto, the man in the lake
eyes those who line the bank
in search of the one already damned.
And what did this young mother see?
Water streaming from the hood.
A bauble clipped to the frame
spruiking colours bright as a carousel
pony. Did someone hold her back?
Did truth unpick her at the seams?

At Her Piano

For Jacinta

Her hands will have to tell the song that plays inside
her head. Her mind is cupped inside the split sphere

of a world I cannot overhear. And all that sounds
is the muffled press of keys as if it were nothing

but a fidget, a distracted tap. Then I turn and watch
her fingers spring from keys like ballerinas spinning

silence back into itself, driving quiet
down so deep it resonates. Her urgent being

sweeps the keys as if to score whales' songs
in seas plumbed to depths beyond my comprehension.

Camels at Eumundi

They sat on the grass, deckchair
    legs tucked under their gut. Necks
        like cobras swung above humps of rough
            carpet. The cut-out cameleer, shapeless

In a seventies kaftan, dragged on
    his cigarette and spat on the lawn. He tilted
        his Akubra and scanned the crowd. The camels
            chewed the cud of their boredom—nomads

Hobbled to a green oval.
    The cartilaginous landscape of their faces
        rippled like a Bedouin desert; eyelashes
            jutted from the lead camel's head, edging

The wet black oases of his eyes. A new clutch
    of riders came, glistening in their awful shorts,
        grins like torn newspaper. They mounted.
            The camels rose like *sadhus*. The riders

Pitched forward then jerked
    backwards—novice cowboys on giant
        rocking horses, joints loosened by the memory
            of treks from the lost city of Ubar

To Damascus trading frankincense,
    or lugging gold from Bambuk in the valley
        of the Senegal to trade for slaves in Timbuktu.
            Their sharp stares shuttled me into the *kilims*

Of their history: the city gates crowded,
    the ninety-nine bastions tinted gold
        by afternoon light—and the caravan laden. Bells
            jangled on tasselled ropes. The clang

Of accoutrements hung in tapestries of dust
    the colour of departure. He led a cortege
        of monotony around the oval, that would-be
            cameleer; and children—one hand on pommels,

The other waving wands
    of fairy floss—festooned the camels' mounds
        like flies. But deep inside those anechoic
            humps—the silent swells of some beheld

Sahara—caravans of camels twelve thousand
    strong haul the accumulated wealth of cruel
        kingdoms along time-honoured trade routes
            —thick with the scent of gentian and fennel

And then the sound: the simoom
    rises, gathers heat from the ground—
        a roiling sprawl of sand, a benighted world.
            On dusk, the rides end, stallholders pack

Boots and box-trailers with clothes racks
    and collapsible pop-ups, and the camels
        wait. Look into their eyes and you'll see it:
            the desert—silent now—its archive plundered.

An Unholy Fire

In the evening they burned the bodies beside
the Ganges. They bound them in white cloth like mummies,
and laid them on top of wood stacks and lit them up.
Incense smoke and candle flame crept
among the weeping relatives wrapped in *puja*[14]
and their best saris, the air gravid with chants
and the clang of drums and bells. Black smoke
drizzled the river past a flotilla of timber
boats painted up like liquorice all-sorts—
tadpole clusters pushing toward the shore—
pregnant with on-lookers. She took us by surprise,
came up behind us as we stood on the ghats and watched
the bodies smoke and burn. Something nudged us:
a struck cadaver dropforged into a bronzed
ruin. Eyes like thin embers burned
in a dish of liquefied flesh. The Ganges seemed
to stop flowing. Water buffalo stalled
in their headlong lurch. We stared at the place where her face
should have been. Instead, a gash, out of which
sound fell. Later, we saw in our mind's
eye an outstretched hand—a flame-hardened
hide wrought to cinder—and we wondered why
we didn't think to fill it with rupees, trying
to avert our eyes from something that could not be.
Yet here it was. She, as if fresh from the flames
of a funeral pyre, the remains of some great
calamity—a conflagration roaring before us.

Minjerribah[15]

Someone's emptied duffle bags of cloud on the horizon
that darken the sea and obscure the island; behind a mist

it's like a zen painting. The ferry surges through a swell
and the island rises before us. Surf breaks white on black

rocks that look like a rent in the ocean's membrane
that could drain the waters of the world. We dock and night

falls fast and the drone of the sea takes us into sleep.
We wake before sunrise. Bush stone-curlews—stiff as nickel

in bark uniforms—post guard on their chicks. Their too-wide
eyes take in shifts of air, of light we can't perceive. Kangaroos

go loose on streets. At South Gorge the sea summons us
and the sun lifts its head from the water and waves unfold

the story of the sea—page after page—as it breaks on rocks,
on our white skin—the murmured history the island wants

to remember, wants to forget. We—foreigners here—
walk a harder shore, the day darkening into us.

That One Day

She rang to ask if I could write a poem
for Australia Day, but not the one you think:
no Union Jacks or bar-b-ques or beers,
or cricket on tv. Normal's taking
place—not here—but somewhere else. It's white,
and it can't see outside itself. It's safe—
for some. It's loud, proclaims itself, denies
the claims of others by its silence. But here,
in a different kind of quiet, an older, darker
story speaks. We'll try to keep our ears,
our minds fast open to the harder truths,
the truths our hearts might recognise at least.
And we might find our grief for what was done—
a smaller grief that tells the larger one.

Breath

The world is still: a held breath against
   the inevitable. Cities slumber on the edge of amnesia.
      Slow streets exhale. Front doors stand open—
         houses comatose. Bus shelters aghast with disuse.

Stop signs stand mute. A swing hangs
   from a dead tree. Crows grapple on greyed limbs.
      Old world henchmen, they fumble in their waiting,
         prophet-clumsy with knowing. The shuttered

Eyes of traffic lights stare down streets
   beyond redemption. No dog barks. No rumour
      rubs the dark hush of the world. A tired wind
         unwinds itself and fades away. Smoke stacks

Perforate a craquelured sky. Sullen air
   slumps against factory walls scrawled with
      bankrupt cant and beyond the blank faces of sky-
         scrapers, clouds calibrate a new ruin. Crow beaks

Click like clap sticks, soothsaying an
   aphotic future. Like an unloved currency,
      the last leaf falls. The earth stops turning, locks onto
         an axis of hopelessness. A breath ends. A shudder

Of discord pulses through the
   universe. The crows shuffle into a new age
      and watch despair ooze across continents like
         an oil spill. At last something is coming to pass.

Dementia, Suburbia

    1

She floods into the café
                  unmoored from the known world,
                                  dragging him
in her wake. On the streets, rain recycles bitumen into oil slicks.
He loses her as she pushes through the crowd milling
at the counter; judgments flash
                      like flares across her bow. Her wet floral
dress strikes an uneasy truce with her crimson gumboots,
an outfit cobbled together because impatience had unmanned

    2

Him on their doorstep that morning. Like every other day
to come she'd struck out into a new world.
                      He'd set the course toward the café;
half way there the clouds broke. Inside she flounders
in friendless waters. Raindrops flick from her hair;
                      her eyes dart from face to face
in search of safe harbour. He stands on the threshold—once
her lighthouse, her Lodestar—as her forgetfulness excises him

3

From this picture. He grabs her hand, pulls her through
the crowd. Abuse shoots from her mouth.
      Enmity swells—silent and spiteful—
a tide she can't perceive. With that slender piece of his mind left
not attending her, he calls his order—a short black, a café latte.
Rain whaling the bitumen
    uncouples her mind. She knows no rest;
her body is an ocean, eternally flowing, receding and flowing.

4

Receding. Receding. It wears her memory down.
He watches her scour the footpath
    as if the mind she'd laid aside had washed ashore
and might be found—hereabouts.
      In streets she knew so well,
it might be put back in her head. He trails her; his hair,
his stained cardigan, speak of things left untended. He waits
for the small joy his coffee will bring.
     She wanders too close to the young

5

Men with polished shoes and clipped
                    beards sitting on milk crates.
He claims her—a lost child—and in doing so, impales
himself on the pointy end
                    of their temper. She maunders
on the footpath, hands outstretched,
                              closing in on ghosts—lamps
flickering in a squall. He leads her away. She looks back
as if she'd forgotten something; he carries the memory
                              of unclaimed coffees

6

Into the downpour. At the lights she tips her face to the rain;
a blue sedan splashes gutter water
                    over them, and a woman in a yellow
coat tries to light a cigarette. A man across the street stares
their way. The chaos of their lives—
                    the minutiae of madness—awaits,
shut up behind a locked front door. She shivers. When he takes
her hand, she looks at him
                    as though she might have known him.

Market Day

I remember the grass pressing
thick beneath my belly on the day
of my birth. A great yellow ball
crept into the sky.
                        The humans
that kept me were kind enough.
They made a fuss when they found me—
a small wet sack nestled into the
paddock. My rough tongue on their
outstretched hands delighted them,
and they named me.
                        The days
passed, and I came to know the
shadows of the trees, the fold and tuck
of pasture, the fence-line, and the dome
of funereal light that came and went
in the night sky. White birds became my
companions. The grass grew me, the
sun drew me into my bullness.
                                    Now
they've sent me from the lick and nuzzle
of my small herd. The monster
I'm crated in roars, slaps me with its iron
hands among the bellows of those who
travel with me.
                    Some think we will
return and stand again up to our bellies
in the water of the dam when the fire ball
burns high in the sky. Some think
nothing. I raise my muzzle to the wind
to see if I can scent the future.

Just One Girl

They hasten into the café dressed
in black, and slide into place at a
table. Their heads dip into menus;
they mention ghosts in their talk.
There's five boys and a single girl
—the numbers stacked against her.
But she ignores the odds, busy
with her phone, deaf to the banter.
She's in a world outside the world
she's in. When she returns—too late
to catch the joke—she smiles
anyway; now they're back on side,
the boys, broadening into a quiet
collegiate pleasure, thinking—one
and all—they have her measure.

Hilltop Station via Wee Jasper

Up in the high country the coats
of cattle thicken toward winter.

Paddocks edged by dark stands
of stringy bark conceal wombat holes

that could snap a horse's leg. A cohort
of boulders loiters near the road like teenagers

in town. The boulders are much older,
cupped in stone skins sloughed off

by the slow work of centuries. One's propped
upright, a misshapen eyeball thumbed

into the pasture and blind to the urgencies
of the world. Old companions, these stones,

they've suffered a long geology together.
Now they nest in the yellow morning

in a fold of paddock, indifferent to the dirt road
that runs past them chasing a destination.

End Game

In the dark—before
    morning stumbles from
        her street swag—you can feel it
            prickling the air's skin. The taste of it—

Sloughed onto dust—settles
    awkwardly on your tongue;
        its scent like creosote burnishes
            the hairs in your nostrils. A hum—

Primordial—embitters
    the wind, and your malleus
        taps it into your inner
            ear. But you sense nothing.

You go about your business
    —set the day in motion—
        reinvesting in the narrative
            you've been feeding yourself

For so long you've forgotten
    where it started. Or why. Or
        because of whom. Hopelessly outside
            yourself, you've harried the world

Into its undoing, into flood
    and ruin, into blame and blood.
        It's too late to say sorry. Be
            calm. Be still. Bear witness.

A Bedroom in Arles

—Vincent van Gogh, Oil on Canvas, 1888

It's small, a set collapsing on itself. Paintings
tilt from walls. Two yellow chairs and a table

make stable something frail. At the head of
the orange bed his coats and hat dangle. A towel

hangs from a nail. A quiet has settled on the clutter
as if each object had quickened into the soft violation

of being watched—our eyes strangers come to rummage
among his personal things. This still life waits

for him to burst in from the wheat fields or le pont
de Langlois. Or from the brothel on Rue du Bout

d'Aeles, where he'd given his ear to Rachel, whom
he loved. Saying *Save it*. But in the bedroom no one

is saved: the doors stay closed, the room unmolested
as lilac walls buckle in the vacuum of his absence.

The Last Moment

IM John Lewis Stacy 1927-2007

He'd been in hospital for eight weeks
when his delirium grew. He talked

to his wife—dead two years now—saying
he'd be home soon. In the evening

he saw cats playing in the corner
of the ward. One night we sat by his bed

and played poker. The cards tipped
into the crevices of the bed linen.

He didn't seem to notice. Dementia
had stolen his poker face. He couldn't

see the pair of queens he held in his hand.
Days passed. He nuzzled unconsciousness,

his body loose with ruin. Disquiet
bloomed on the white walls. On the last

day he snatched his daughter's hand
and held it to his chest. An amulet.

Only when his breathing stopped
did she feel the slackness come.

Bull

The bull settled his bulk
into the lap of the paddock,

his monumental ease
nestled between the atmosphere

and the slow curve of the earth.
In the pods of his eyes

the dam lay flat.
His half-ton head swung

in the gloaming, horns
thick as a man's arm.

Mist streamed from his muzzle.
A thunderous bellow, loosed

from the depths of his belly—
that harbourage of draughts

and slaughter—called the night down.
And the full moon—another wild eye—

came flying over the unfenced
fields of his omnipotence.

The Woman on the Bus

Under the airport terminal's low brow,
we sit on a bus and wait for a passenger,
the air stiff with impatience.
                         Across the tarmac
the Rex Airlines plane gleams ready
in the muted light. Baggage cars
clamour past. Jets taxi through
a sky distilling rain. Nearby buses
fume the air.
             Across the aisle, two
women sit, one in her forties, the other
sixty odd. They share some acquaintance,
they find. The younger one asks, 'So how
have you been?' The lines in the older
woman's face deepen. 'Not great,' she says.
'I'm coming home from my daughter's funeral.'
A bus full of heads click still.
The sound of the engine idling becomes
an opera of uncertainty. 'I'm sorry,'
the younger woman says, her eyes fixed
on the older woman's face. The older
woman looks down at the hands she cups
in her lap; she picks at the floral
pattern of her dress. 'We don't know
how she died.'
              The late passenger—
a man in a suit—steps into the bus.
The silence thickens like a stew. Like
a child admonished for being late to Sunday
School, he takes a seat. He puts his brief
case at his feet and parts a daily paper;
it crumples like tin. The bus leaves.
                              The passengers

withdraw into their worlds. The younger
woman gazes out the window at
an empty tarmac, wondering which weighs
heavier: the loss or not knowing why.

Awake to the Rest of My Days

Morning strolls the horizon, folding
               up clouds and putting them into the sky's
blue wardrobes. I've woken to the rest of my days.
The sun—a young prince—cartwheels on the grass
despite himself, the lilly pilly gilding him with crimson
fruit. The sky yawns:
               a god waking from fresh-made love and I—
a grifter—wait around the corner
                       of my life, trying to bilk time

as it spills through my fingers
               like milk. I lug my body
onto the forecourt of the morning in the hope the sun
might soak some
        sense into me. The world is the wind,
the night cries of the curlew, the ocean's slow retreat
from the shore; it's what remains
               after time has hung me out to dry,
and the hours and years I've been gifted
             pass inside the shadow of themselves.

Epilogue

Winter Lamb

For my brother Bernie

She rose from frozen ground on bony legs
—wet with birth—and stumbled onto the road.
Sleet swept the paddocks. The cord's shrivelled
end scraped the dirt as she leaned into
me, and pressed a patch of urine—flecked
with blood—onto my jeans. I rang my brother.
Yeah, he said. Just leave it there.
                                    The ewes
mobbed on the far side of the paddock, still
as granite. I walked the bend in the road. My brother
—in the distance—crossed to the kennels, fattened
by his jacket, a swarm of dogs around
his legs. Too cold for lambs this time of year,
he said, phone jammed between ear and shoulder.
He scooped food into each dog's dish and locked
them up as he went. They might come back for it,
he said, meaning the ewes. He saw the weather
closing in and drew his hand to wave
me on and walked towards the house; the wind
banged the door; its echo reckoned the gap
between us as it met me at the grid.
Sleet turned to snow. The darkening air
poached the light from the kitchen; the chimney
loosed bridles of white into the sky.

Notes

Watercourses, p. 29:
[1] The phrase 'snug as guns' is an adulteration of Seamus Heaney's line 'snug as a gun' in his poem 'Digging' from *Death of a Naturalist (1966)*.

My Grandmother's Voice, The Rain, p. 32:
[2] ' … another world entire.' From Cormac McCarthy's *The Crossing* (1994) p. 4.

Thirty Years On, p. 38:
[3] After Ted Kooser's poem, *Father*. I've borrowed and inverted his first line, 'Today you'd be ninety-seven if you had lived.'

Last We Heard, p. 39:
[4] A line borrowed from Rupi Kaur, *Milk and Honey* (2014), p. 52.

He on the Earth of the Night, p. 45:
[5] After Dylan Thomas, *Poem on his Birthday*.
[6] A phrase unconsciously borrowed from Seamus Heaney's poem *North*: ' … and found only the secular/powers of the Atlantic thundering.'
[7] The phrase alludes to a line in the G M Hopkins poem, *As Kingfishers Catch Fire*: ' … *myself* it speaks and spells/ Crying *What I do is me: for that I came*.'

No Southern Boobook, p. 57:
[8] after Bronwyn Lea's poem *The Island is Different Now*.

Death in the Afternoon, p. 64:
[9] After Ernest Hemingway, 'Death in the Afternoon' (1932).

A Waking Dream, p. 69:
[10] From *Bright Star* by John Keats: ' … to feel forever its soft fall and swell … '.

Now What, p. 71:
[11] From *Sunday Night*, by Raymond Carver.

Portrait of a Young Adventurer, p. 72:
[12] *salwar kurta*: A suit comprising loose-fitting pants and a loose shirt falling about the knees, traditionally worn by men.

Late Night Poem, p. 83:
[13] Echoes the line: 'But trailing clouds of glory do we come … ' from Wordsworth's *Ode 536: Intimations of Immortality from Recollections of Early Childhood*.

An Unholy Fire, p. 91:
[14] *puja*: Hindi, 'prayer'.

Minjerribah, p. 92:
[15] Local Jandai language name for Stradbroke Island, meaning 'Island in the Sun'.

About the Author

Kevin Smith lived in a sawmill village, and grew up on the western edge of the Snowy Mountains in NSW. He has worked primarily in drama and theatre, as actor and writer, and taught in high school, TAFE and university. His poems have been published here and overseas: in England, Wales, Ireland and the US. In Australia, he's had poems published in the Newcastle (2018, 2021) the ACU (2021), and the Grieve (2020) Poetry Prize Anthologies. Poems have been published in *The Hinterland Times* and in *Newsmonth*, the Australian Independent Education Union magazine. His poems have been runners-up, finalists, short-listed, gained special mentions, commended, and honourable mentions in major competitions in Australia and overseas. He reads his work regularly at Outspoken in Maleny, and was a regular reader at SpeedPoets in Brisbane. His poems have been heard at the Woodford Festival, and various venues on the Sunshine Coast. Mark Tredinnick says Kevin's 'is a rare voice in Australian poetry … [His poems] remind us what poetry is for.'

www.kevinsmithpoetry.com

www.ingramcontent.com/pod-product-compliance
Lightning Source LLC
Chambersburg PA
CBHW051601010526
44118CB00023B/2779